DISCOVER HAWAI'I'S NATURAL FORESTS
Written by David Boynton
Illustrated by Katherine Orr

Originally published by

ISLAND HERITAGE
PUBLISHING

Reprinted in 2020 by Katherine Orr
with permission from Island Heritage.
For educational use.

Please address orders and correspondence to:

Katherine Orr
44-119 Bayview Haven Place
Kaneohe, HI 96744, USA
(808) 234-5508 www.katherineshelleyorr.com

Copyright © 2020 by Katherine S. Orr
All rights reserved. Portions of this book may be
reproduced and modified for educational
purposes with permission from the author.
Printed in the USA

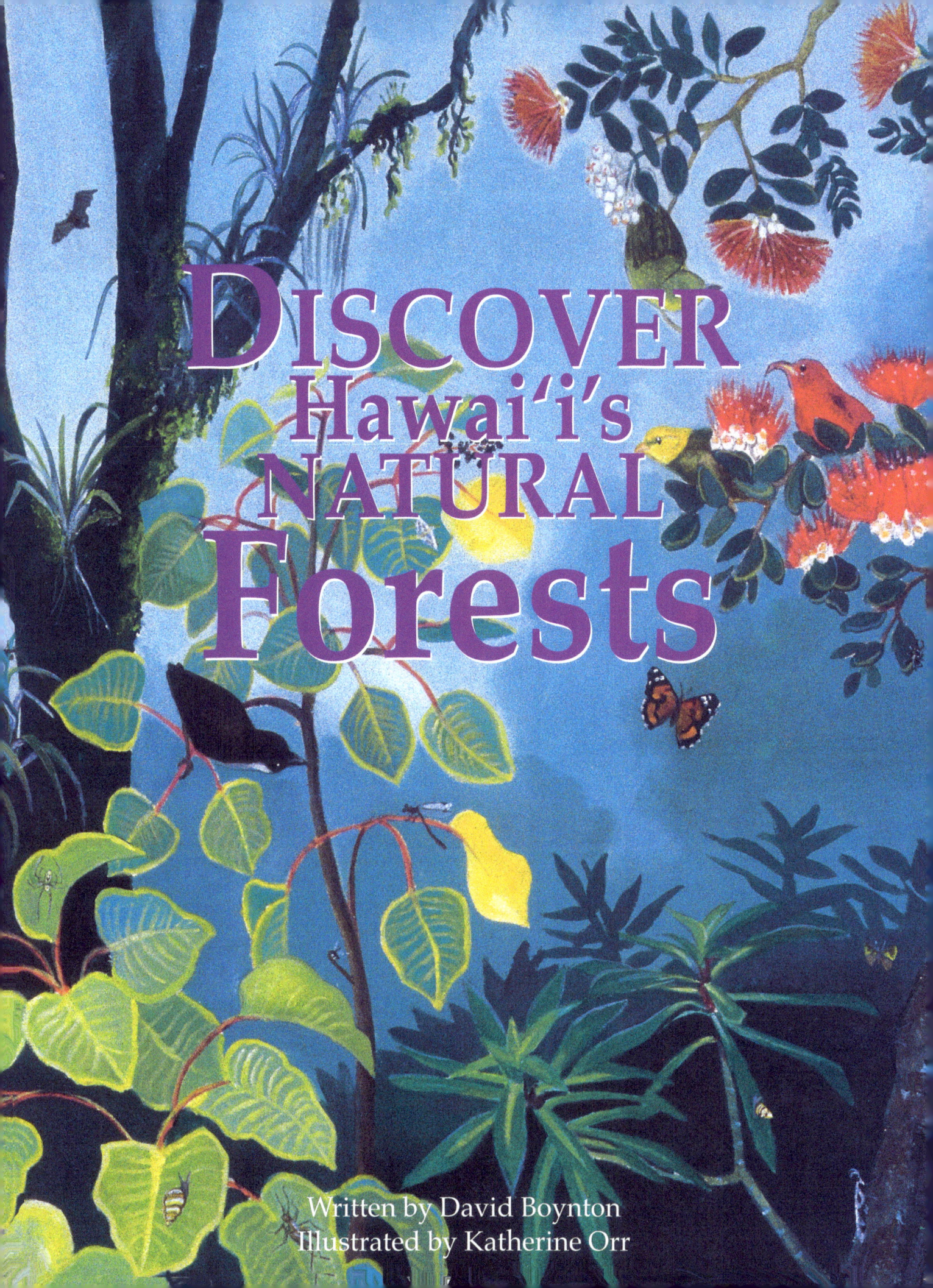

CONTENTS

Introduction 3
A Hawaiian Forest Is Born: Life on Lava 4
The Arrival of Life (Wind, Wings, Waves) 6
Endemic Species: Made in Hawai'i 7
What is a Forest? 8
Ferns and Mosses 10
Shrubs 12
Insects: Carnivorous Caterpillars and Happy-face Spiders 14
Tree Snails and Land Snails 16
Birds 18
Layers of Life in the Forest 22
Forest Zones 24
Shrublands 26
Dryland Forests 26
The Moist Forest 28
The Rainforest 29
Bogs 30
Sub-alpine Forest 31
Alien Plants from Around The World 32
Polynesian Introductions 34
Threats and Challenges 36
Endangered Species 38
Caring for Our Forests: What You Can Do to Help 41
Glossary 42
Index 44

INTRODUCTION

Swirling mists float through moss-covered branches. Countless leaves dance with the wind in ever-changing patterns of green and yellow. Standing high on a mountain slope, surrounded by forest, at first you see only plants, but then you look more closely... Along the edge of a leaf, a tiny green caterpillar stands upright and still. Smaller than a blade of grass, it looks like part of the leaf itself until a tiny fly lands nearby. In the blink of an eye, the caterpillar twists and grabs the fly between sharp claws. Calmly, it begins to eat the fly head first.

Hawai'i's carnivorous caterpillars live only in these forests, along with many other insects, birds and plants found nowhere else on earth. Come and meet other members of this special world as we explore the wonders of Hawai'i's natural forests.

A Hawaiian Forest Is Born: Life on Lava

Each Hawaiian island began life naked as a newborn baby, with no covering of plants. The Big Island of Hawai'i is still being "born" as flowing streams of lava cool and harden into bare rock. With little shelter or shade, this is not an easy place for plants to grow, yet grow they will. In some places gray and white lichens (LI-kens) cover the new lava, and rows of ferns spring from cracks which offer both shade and moisture.

Tiny seeds from *'ōhi'a lehua* trees and *'ōhelo* bushes settle and sprout, and soon the fields of lava are dotted with small bushes. As leaves fall and lava slowly breaks down, soil begins to form, allowing other plants to take root. Where once there was bare rock, a forest is born.

The Arrival of Life (Wind, Wings, Waves)

Plants that colonize a new place are called *pioneers*. Whether on a new lava flow, a sandy beach or an uninhabited island, they must be strong to survive. The pioneer plants that colonize new lava flows on the Big Island of Hawai'i haven't far to travel. They come from the nearby fields and forests. But those pioneers that are first to settle on a new island must survive a long journey under difficult conditions before reaching land.

Some pioneers arrive by wind. Strong winds called the jet stream are blowing high above us all the time at 60 miles per hour and more. A scientist who wanted to find out if these winds could carry life across the ocean once attached a large funnel-shaped net to an airplane and flew at over 30,000 feet to find out. He collected hundreds of spores, seeds, and insects floating on these high-in-the-sky winds. He even collected small spiders that sailed on the wind like tiny kites by dangling a long thread of web behind them.

Some birds arrive on an island because they are blown off course during storms, while other birds flock to the islands each winter like tourists to enjoy the warm climate. Sometimes these birds carry hitchhikers - seeds stuck in their feathers or on muddy feet. In their stomachs, they may also carry seeds which they drop off in a little pile of fertilizer upon reaching land.

Ocean waves and currents also carry plants and animals to new land. Most seeds would be long-dead after being thrashed by waves, soaked in salt water, then tossed up on a beach to roast in the sun. But some seeds have such hard shells, or *seed coats*, that they can survive for months floating on the ocean. At times, entire trees are carried off to sea by storms, becoming rafts for insects, snails, seeds, and whatever other life may cling to their branches as they drift to new land.

ENDEMIC SPECIES: MADE IN HAWAI'I

When the first Polynesian voyaging canoes reached these islands, what plants did they find here? They did not find bananas, mangoes or papayas. There were no guavas and probably not even coconuts! Most of the fruits and vegetables we eat today, as well as the flowers, shrubs and trees we see around our neighborhoods, were brought to these islands by people. What plants were already here? Head to the forests and you will see. Most of Hawai'i's native plants and animals - those that arrived without help from people - are found in Hawai'i's natural forests. And most of these native species are found nowhere else on earth.

About one thousand different types of flowering plants are native to Hawai'i. More than 900 of these native plants are *endemic* - found only in Hawai'i and nowhere else. Some are endemic to several islands, others to just one island, and many are endemic to just part of an island. These endemic species are special because Hawai'i is their only home.

How did these endemic species come to be? The Hawaiian Islands have many different environments: hot, dry sand dunes; cool, lush rainforests; steep, narrow valleys; wide mountain slopes; rocky cliff faces; salt-sprayed seashores; swampy bogs; and freezing cold mountains more than two miles high. Pioneer plants that settled on Hawai'i's islands long ago spread their seeds across many different places. Over tens of thousands of years these plants *evolved*, or changed, into new forms that could survive in these different environments.

WHAT IS FOREST?

If you described a forest as a big patch of trees you would not be wrong, but a forest is also much more than trees. It includes all forms of life that live there: mosses, fungi, bushes, vines, birds, snails, spiders, and insects by the thousands. Hawai'i's forests are filled with dozens of types of birds, hundreds of snails, and thousands of insects that are found nowhere else. Because they evolved together, these special Hawaiian species depend on one another to survive. The plants need certain birds and insects to pollinate their flowers; the birds and insects need certain plants for food and shelter. Far more than a large bunch of trees, a healthy forest is made up of hundreds of different plants and animals living and working together in many different ways. Because so many of Hawai'i's forest species are endemic, Hawai'i's native forests are truly like no other forests in the world.

1. 'elepaio
2. Hawaiian bat
3. Blackburn's butterfly
4. pa'iniu
5. pueo
6. puaiohi
7. pomace fly
8. happy-face spider
9. tree snail
10. tree cricket
11. geometrid moth
12. 'ōlapa tree
13. po'ouli
14. damselfly
15. carnivorous caterpillar
16. na'ena'e
17. case-bearer micromoth
18. green spirit moth
19. Kaua'i weevil
20. Kamehameha butterfly
21. 'ō'ū
22. 'i'iwi
23. 'alauahio
24. 'ōhi'a lehua tree

FERNS AND MOSSES?

Stand deep in the rainforest and look around. You'll notice that you can't even see the trunks of trees. They are hidden beneath thick, spongy layers of mosses and ferns. Little worlds of life hide in and around these tiny gardens of ferns and mosses, so beautiful in the rays of sunlight that filter down through the forest.

Look closely at a clump of moss and notice that it looks like tiny ferns. Most ferns are larger than mosses, sometimes MUCH larger. *Hāpu'u 'i'i*, the tallest Hawaiian tree fern, grows

spikemoss

finger fern

false staghorn fern

tongue fern

lace fern *sword fern*

as high as a two-story building, with fronds (leaves) that are fifteen feet long! Do you think you could recognize ferns that have shapes like their names, such as tongue, lace, staghorn, finger, and sword ferns?

Ferns and mosses do not produce seeds as flowering plants do. Instead, they reproduce by tiny spores the size of dust. Mosses grow little hairs that stand upright, holding small spore cups, each filled with hundreds of spores that are spread by wind and rain. Ferns also have spore cups, or *sori* (pronounced sore-eye). Look for them on the underside of the fern leaf. They come in spots and dots and rows of all shapes and sizes. You can recognize different ferns by the patterns of their sori.

SHRUBS

Shrubs and other small plants fill the spaces between the forest's taller trees. In dry parts of the islands, there were once large patches of shrubs with almost no trees, called *shrublands*. Very little remains of Hawai'i's native shrublands due to wildfires, clearing for sugar and pineapple plantations, and damage from cattle that were brought to the islands more than 200 years ago.

Many forest shrubs are used to make beautiful necklaces called *lei*. Two common shrubs, *'a'ali'i* and *pūkiawe*, are still used today by lei makers. Other shrubland plants such as *ko'oko'olau* and *'uhaloa* are used for medicine. People collect the leaves of *ko'oko'olau* for a medicinal tea, and the root bark of *'uhaloa* for sore throat, just as Hawaiians have done for hundreds of years.

Certain Hawaiian shrubs are of great interest to scientists around the world, especially the *silverswords* and *lobelias* (lo-BEEL-ya). Silverswords grow at high elevations on Maui and

koli'i

greensword

ahinahina (Haleakalā silversword)

i'iwi's bill fits the curve of a lobelioid flower

the Big Island where sunlight is very strong. The silvery hairs covering the silversword's leaves act like mirrors that reflect the bright light and protect the leaves from sunburn. More than 30 relatives of the silversword have evolved in Hawai'i and are found nowhere else. They live in many different environments, including dry forests, rainforests and bogs. Most are called greenswords, because they lack the silver color of their high elevation cousins.

There are more than one hundred different kinds of Hawaiian lobelia, and all are found only in Hawai'i. About ninety of these evolved from just one ancestor. Many have curved flowers that are a perfect fit for the bills of Hawaiian honeycreepers, a group of birds that includes the bright red 'i'iwi. When the 'i'iwi dips its bill into the lobelia flower to sip its sweet nectar, a spot of pollen rubs off on the bird's forehead. When the bird visits the next lobelia flower, pollen from the first flower rubs off on the second one and fertilizes it. Good teamwork!

INSECTS: CARNIVOROUS CATERPILLARS AND HAPPY-FACE SPIDERS

For millions of years before people came to the Hawaiian Islands, there were no frogs or other amphibians, no lizards or other reptiles, and only one land mammal - ʻōpeʻapeʻa - the Hawaiian bat. Insects were the rulers of the animal world, but not the common insects we see around our homes, for there were no house flies, no roaches, no ants, no mosquitoes, and no honeybees. Instead, there were thousands of endemic insects that are unique to Hawaiʻi. To find them today, the best place to look is in Hawaiʻi's native forests.

Insects belong to a group of joint-legged animals, called *arthropods*, that includes crabs, shrimp, and spiders. Most of Hawaiʻi's native insects live on land, some live in fresh water, and a few live on both land and water. Hawaiʻi's largest insect is *pinao*, a bright blue dragonfly which feeds on other flying insects. While adult *pinao* live on land, their larvae, or young, live in streams where they catch insects and small fish for food.

A set of pale purple wings the size of your fingernail flutters from flower to flower. It's Blackburn's butterfly, one of only two butterflies native to Hawaiʻi. The other

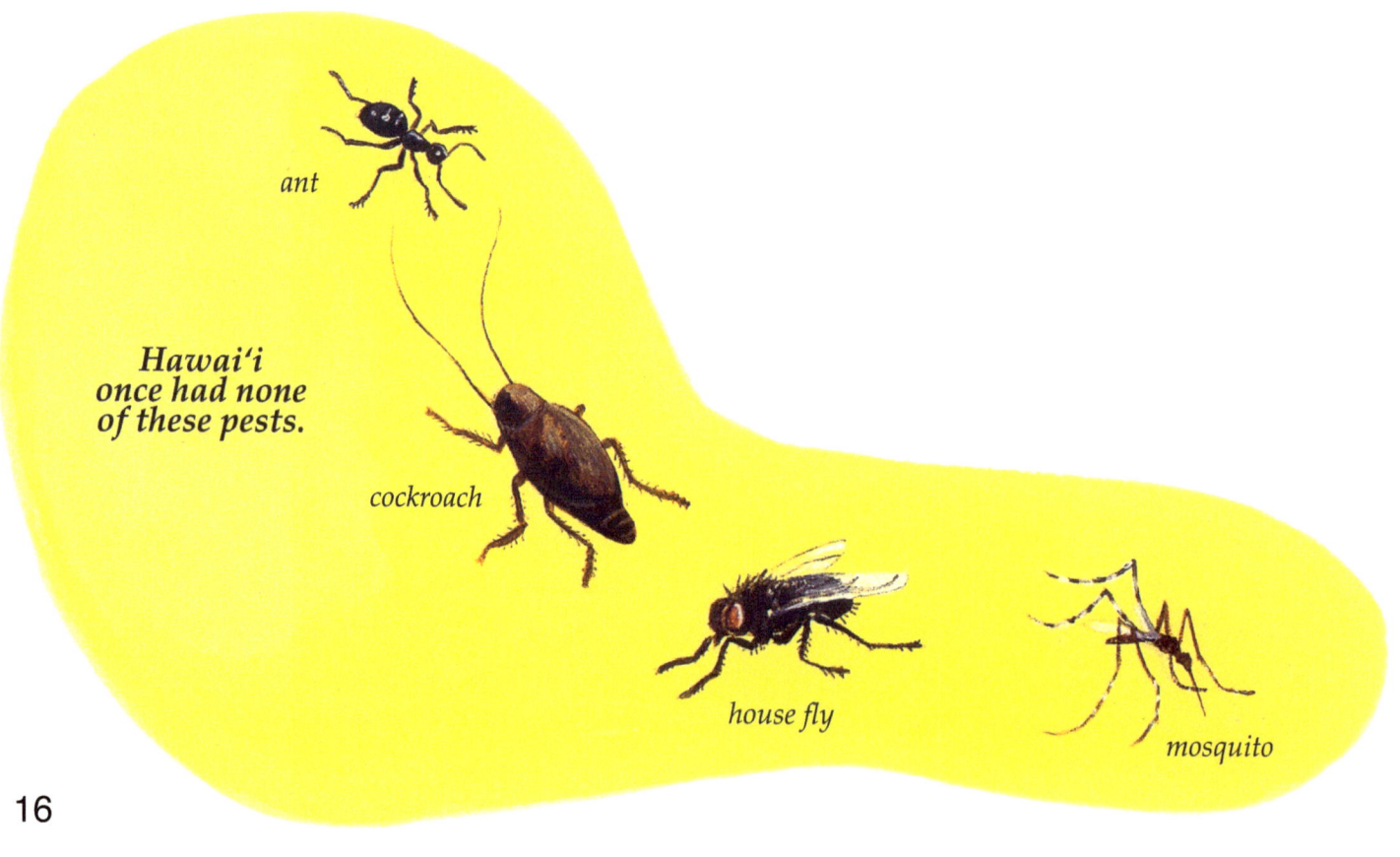

Hawaiʻi once had none of these pests.

ant

cockroach

house fly

mosquito

pinao

Hawaiian happy-face spider

Kamehameha caterpillars have been munching their lunch.

Perhaps the most famous of Hawai'i's miniature wildlife is a little spider with a big smile. The "happy-face" spider has pale yellow legs and a body about the size of this "O." What looks like a smile are red and black markings on the spider's back. No one knows for sure why the happy face spider wears a clown-like smile on its back, but one guess is that the patterns help to camouflage the spider as it hides under leaves in the native forests on O'ahu, Moloka'i, Maui, and the Big Island.

Hawai'i has nearly 20 types of carnivorous caterpillars, each with different camouflage. One is green and hides on leaf edges; another is pale brown like a tiny twig; a spotted bristly green one hides in moss on tree trunks, and another brown one blends in with the surrounding dead leaves. Although the moths of these caterpillars had been known for years, scientists were quite amazed to discover caterpillars that can ambush living insects as their prey.

Kamehameha butterfly

Blackburn's butterfly

carnivorous caterpillar and its moth

Tree Snails and Land Snails

It's hard to imagine how little land snails the size of your fingertip could cross 2,000 miles of ocean and survive. But reach Hawai'i they did - long before people ever arrived - and evolved into more than 1,000 endemic species that are found nowhere else. Most are rather small and plain looking, although scientists find them interesting. For example, when archaeologists study places where ancient Hawaiians lived for hundreds of years, they can tell how the forest environment changed by the types of snails they find there.

Largest of these land snails were the Carelia, found on Kaua'i. Some lived in the forest, others lived under the rocks or talus that collects at the base of cliffs. No living Carelia

Fossil shells of Carelia and other land snails

Colorful shells of Hawai'i's tree snails

have been found for over 40 years, and they are probably now all extinct. However, the 2-3 inch snail shells are still found in old soil or sand deposits, stream beds, and along cliffs. Maybe someday a careful observer will find a living Carelia snail!

Seeing one of O'ahu's colorful tree snails is like finding a little gem in the forest. The ancient Hawaiians called them *pupu kani oe*, the singing snails, but scientists say the sound comes from crickets singing in the forest. They are also known as *kahuli*, which means "to turn over" or "to search," and that's what they do as they crawl over and under leaves in the native forest. Adult snails give birth to just one or two young each year, so the snail's population is slow to grow.

BIRDS

Red like *lehua* flowers, green and yellow as sunlit leaves, brown like the bark of trees, or black as the forest shadows . . . dozens of endemic birds make their home in Hawai'i's forests. You may hear their song while hiking in the mountains, but it's not easy to see them. If you're patient and can find what they like to feed on - perhaps an *'ōhi'a lehua* tree full of flowers or a grove of *koa* trees - you'll be rewarded with a look at birds that few people get to see.

Kaua'i amakihi

po'ouli

'i'iwi

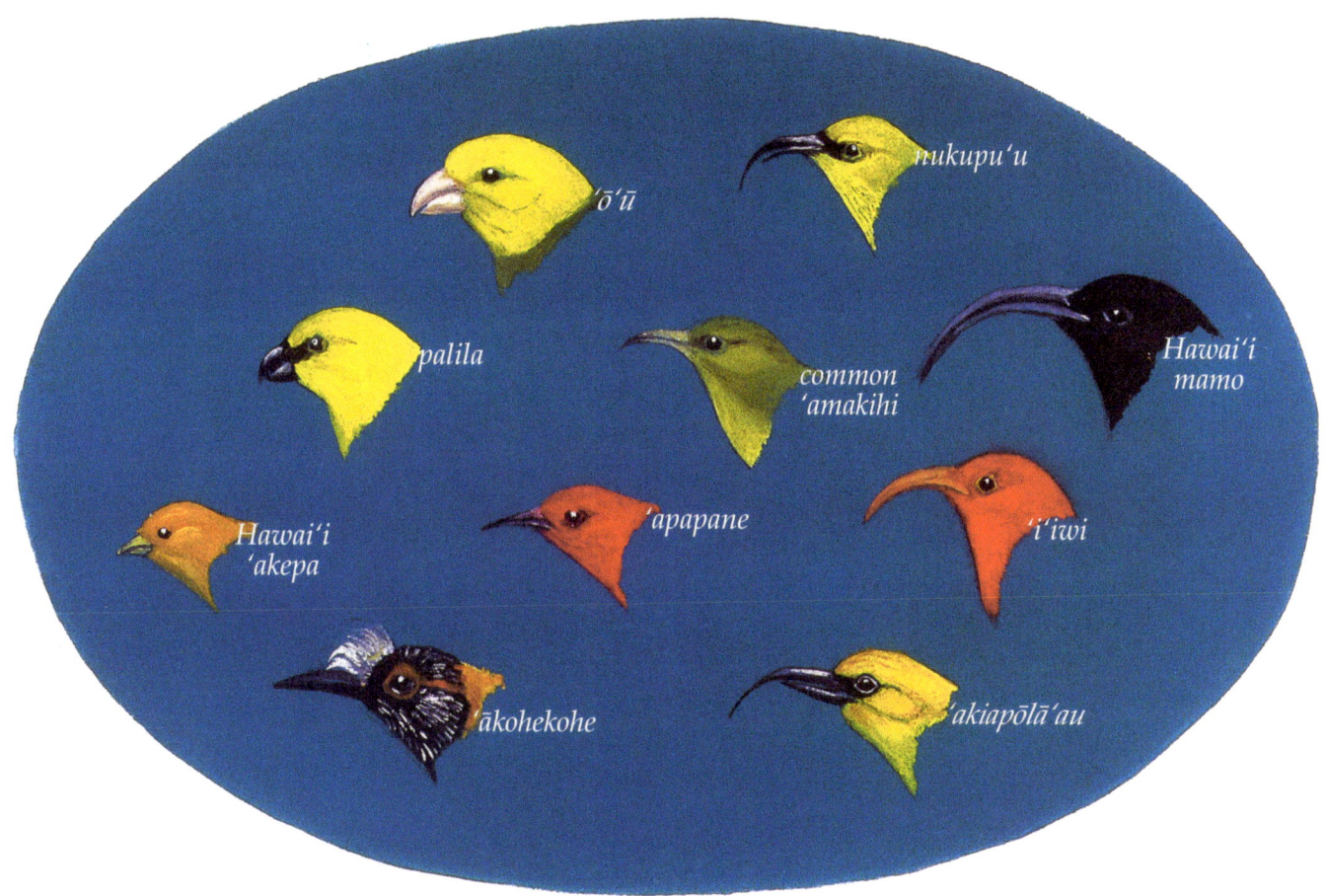

Birders from around the world are fascinated by Hawai'i's honeycreepers. This group of birds is one of the best examples of a type of evolution known as *adaptive radiation*, which means that many different species evolved from one ancestor.

The ancestors, perhaps a pair or a small flock of birds, looked like house finches or sparrows, which have short, cone-shaped beaks. From these evolved honeycreepers with slightly-curved, steeply-curved and long-curved beaks, short and narrow beaks, wide and thick beaks, and parrot-like beaks. One of the most unusual honeycreepers, the *akiapōlā'au*, uses its straight lower beak to hammer like a woodpecker but has a curved upper beak for picking out small insect larvae.

Honeycreepers can live together in the forest because they don't all do the same thing. For example, they nest in different places, and have different ways of feeding. Some have long curved beaks that can pry under moss and rotting branches for insects; others have shorter curved beaks that fit right into curved flowers, thick curved beaks for eating fruit, thick pointed beaks for breaking open seeds, and short beaks for eating insects. Some species such as *'apapane* and *'amakihi* have slightly-curved beaks that do a little bit of everything.

A little brown and gray bird with a perky tail comes hopping over and under branches until it's so close you can almost touch it. It's the ʻelepaio, our friendliest native forest bird. ʻElepaio are in the Flycatcher family and eat only insects.

For the Hawaiians of old, ʻelepaio was the guardian of the canoe-maker, or kahuna kālai waʻa. When a huge koa tree was found, the kahuna kālai waʻa would wait for the ʻelepaio. If the ʻelepaio came to the tall koa and stayed for a while to feed, the kahuna would leave the tree in the forest, saying it belonged to the bird. This was a smart thing to do, as ʻelepaio enjoy trees that have rotten wood full of insects to eat, and such a tree would not make a very good canoe.

Red feathers from ʻiʻiwi, green from ʻoʻu and other birds, black and yellow feathers from mamo and ʻōʻō - all were prized feathers collected for the aliʻi (chiefs) of ancient Hawaiʻi. They were used to make lei, helmets, idols, and spectacular feather cloaks. One great cape made for King Kamehameha used the feathers from 80,000 birds, collected over many, many years.

Just a few feathers were picked off of some birds like the ʻōʻō, and the bird was then released to live on. Almost all the feathers were taken from other birds such as the ʻiʻiwi, and what was left became food for the bird catchers. Carefully tied in small clumps with strong olonā fibers, the feathers blend together like soft velvet. The capes have lasted for hundreds of years, and are among the most highly-prized creations of the ancient Hawaiians.

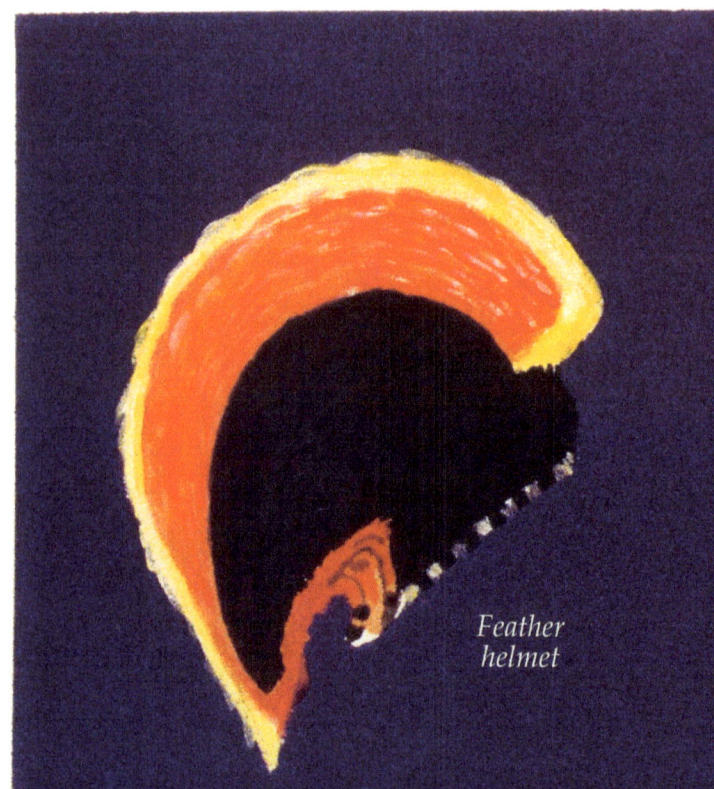

Feather helmet

Thousands of feathers adorn capes and cloaks worn by Hawai'i's ali'i

LAYERS OF LIFE IN THE FOREST

*D*eep in a Hawaiian forest, mosses and ferns surround you, larger ferns and shrubs shade you, and far above your head, tall trees spread their leafy branches against the sky. Forest floor, understory, and canopy - these layers of the forest create many different *habitats*, or homes, for all who live there.

Looking up at the *canopy* of a *koa* forest is like looking at the sky through a huge covering of lace. Little spots of green, red, or yellow flit from branch to branch, as honeycreepers search for food high above. It is shady under the forest canopy - a cool environment for the many plants of the understory and forest floor, and a cool place where people can hike, relax, and enjoy the beauty of nature.

Bushes, shrubs, and small trees fill the middle forest layer, or *understory*, offering a rich and varied habitat for insects and birds to feed, hide, and nest. Tropical rainforests in other parts of the world often have *liana*, or large vines, hanging throughout the understory, but the vines in Hawai'i's forests are quite small.

Fallen leaves, branches, and tree trunks end up on the *forest floor*. Slowly but surely they are broken down, returning their nutrients to the soil. If you were to turn over some of the leaf litter, you would find tiny scurrying insects, burrowing earthworms, and fungi that help to *decompose* the compost.

All around are ferns, mosses, and small shrubs. Some grow from the ground while others sprout from living or dead trees. Each has a special beauty for those who take the time to look. When it rains, the floor of a healthy natural forest is like a giant sponge, soaking up water into the ground. Eventually, it will become *groundwater* and later our drinking water when we pump it back up to the surface through wells.

CANOPY

UNDERSTORY

FOREST FLOOR

25

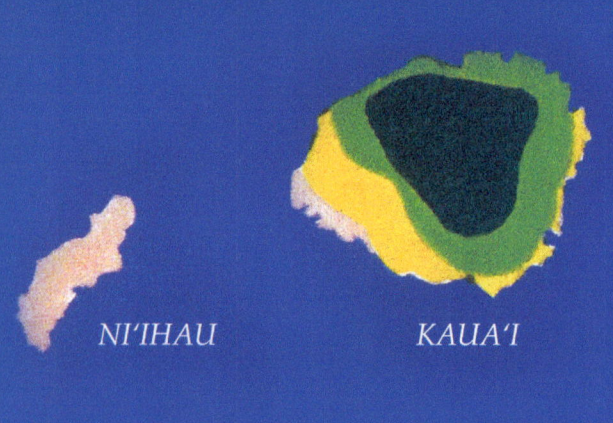

NI'IHAU KAUA'I

O'AHU

FOREST ZONES

There are many different kinds of Hawaiian forests, one type blending into another. Variations in temperature and rainfall help create these different forests.

As you travel from the shoreline up the mountain slopes the air becomes cooler and rainfall increases, resulting in different forest zones. Low elevation grasslands and shrublands gradually change to dryland forest, and then to moist or mesic forest where Hawaiian *koa* trees are the dominant (most common) tree. The rainiest parts of the islands are usually between 4,000 - 6,000 feet elevation, about one mile high above sea level. Here you'll find the rainforest zone, where *'ōhi'a lehua* is the dominant tree. Hawai'i has the only tropical rainforests in our 50 states.

On the islands of Maui and the Big Island, the mountains are much higher than on the other islands, reaching over 10,000 feet above sea level on Haleakalā, and over 13,000 feet on Mauna Kea and Mauna Loa. The temperature becomes cooler as you travel up these high mountains, and there is less rainfall the higher you go.

In some areas above the rainforest there is a zone of tall *koa* trees. On the Big Island, the yellow-flowered *māmane* tree creates a unique high elevation forest, which you can see if you drive over the Saddle Road between Mauna Kea and Mauna Loa. Gradually, the trees become shorter, until once again shrublands dominate the landscape of the sub-alpine zone. At the top of the highest mountains is the cold, dry, alpine zone where very few plants can survive.

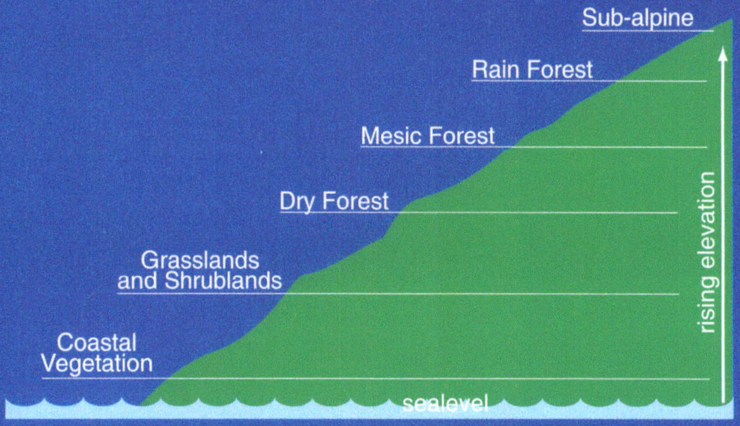

LEEWARD (WESTWARD) FOREST ZONES

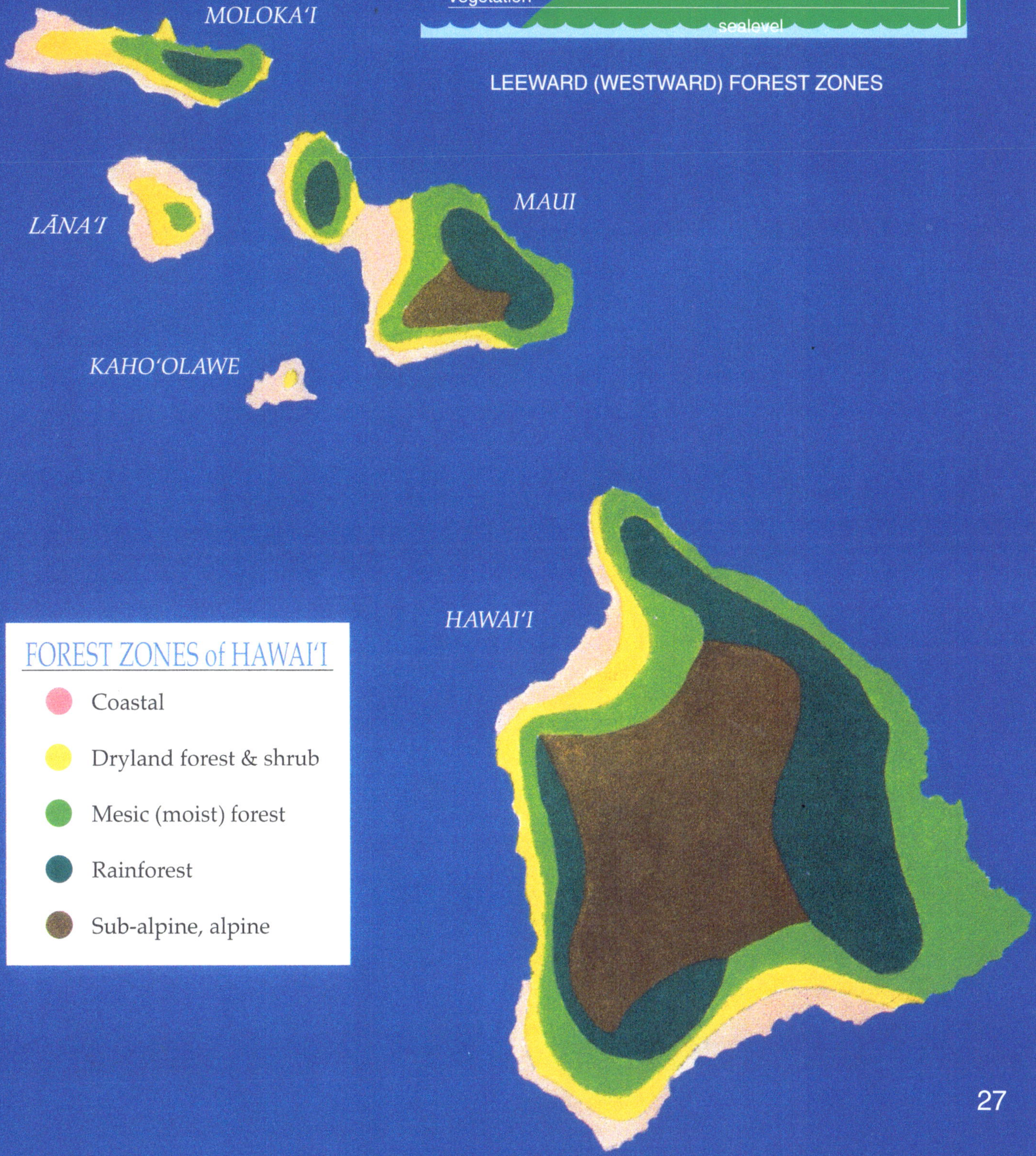

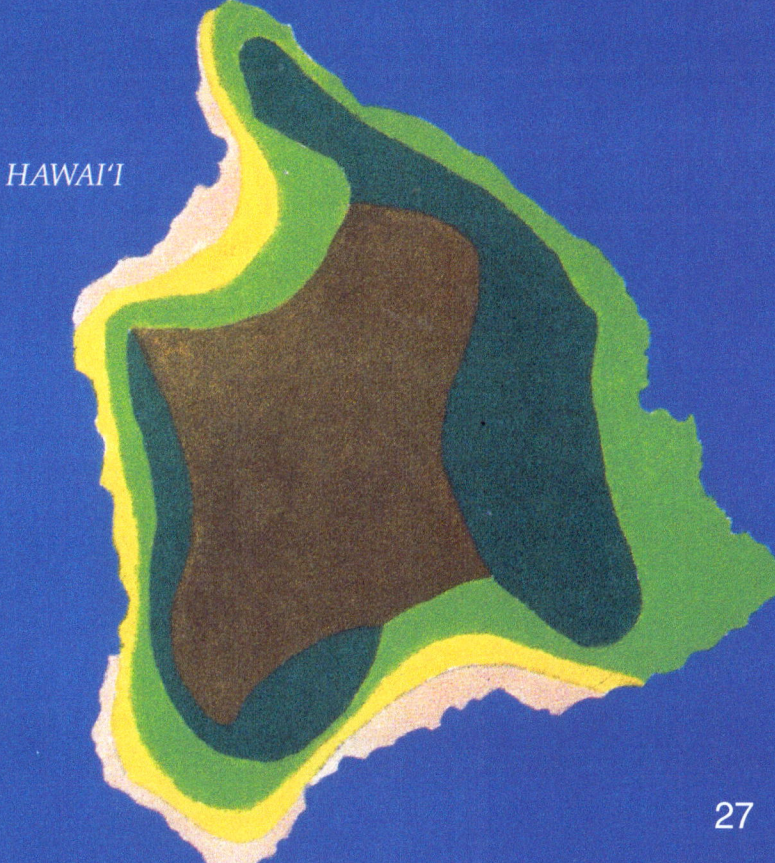

SHRUBLANDS

Today, much of Hawai'i's lowland mountain slopes are covered either by pineapple and cane fields, or housing. In times of old, however, shrublands and grasslands covered much of the lowland landscape, especially on the drier leeward side of the islands. Here, *pili* grass was abundant, and very important to the Hawaiians who collected large bundles of it to make their homes.

DRYLANDS FORESTS

If you were ever lost in the desert, you would learn very quickly how important it is to conserve water. Plants of Hawai'i's dryland forests need to conserve water too. The *wiliwili* tree does this by losing all its leaves during the dry season. Later, beautiful flowers that may be white, yellow or orange sprout, and these will turn into "bean" pods with bright red seeds.

Growing in dryland forests on the Big Island are two kinds of trees with very dense wood that will sink like a rock if dropped into water. The rarest is *uhiuhi*, a small tree with black wood that is very hard and heavy. *Kauila*, a larger tree, also inhabits dryland forests. *Uhiuhi* and the Big Island *kauila* are both listed as endangered species. Ancient Hawaiians made *'o'o* or digging sticks from *kauila*, as well as spears and *kapa* beaters.

Several extremely rare hibiscus relatives live in dryland forests. *Hibiscadelphus* trees have yellow-green, funnel-shaped flowers that are probably pollinated by birds or moths. *Koki'o* or "tree-cottons" have large, bright orange-red flowers and leaves shaped like *kukui* tree leaves. The rarest *koki'o* is the Moloka'i species. At one time, all that was left in the world were a couple of branches of a Moloka'i *koki'o* that had been grafted onto a different species. Through culture of individual cells from these branches, scientists have been able to create new plants to be returned to the wild.

koa tree

THE MOIST FOREST

Between the dryland and rainforest zones is the moist or *mesic* forest, where *koa* is king. It's a beautiful forest of tall trees with wide spreading branches that form a lace-like canopy against the sky. Beneath the shady canopy is a mix of smaller trees and shrubs in the understory.

Koa forest is excellent habitat for native wildlife. Insect life is abundant, and this in turn provides food for native forest birds such as ʻamakihi, ʻiʻiwi, and ʻelepaio. Sit still in the *koa* forest and you may see them flit from branch to branch searching for insects.

Straight, tall *koa* trees were highly valued by the Hawaiians of old, just as they are today by modern woodworkers. *Koa* wood has lots of color and a beautiful grain. Although much of Hawaiʻi's *koa* forests have been lost to logging, pasture, and farming, foresters and woodworkers are interested in replanting *koa* trees on lands where sugarcane is no longer grown.

THE RAINFOREST

Squeeze the moss covering the tree trunks and water will ooze out as if you had squeezed a sponge. Ferns are everywhere, covering the ground and sprouting as *epiphytes* (EH-pi-fites) in trees. Here, tree trunks are covered so thickly with moss that you can't even see their bark. This is the rainforest, where rainfall averages over 100 inches per year. If you spend a day in the rainforest, it is very likely that you'll be walking in the clouds, and you'd better have rain gear; whether you pick a *lehua* flower or not, there's a good chance it will rain!

'Apapane and other native forest birds sip nectar from the bright red flowers of *'ōhi'a lehua*, the most abundant tree in the rainforest. *'Ōlapa* and *lapalapa* trees are also plentiful, their thin-stemmed leaves dancing on the slightest forest breeze.

Because of bird diseases carried by mosquitoes, many native forest birds have disappeared from lower elevation forests. Today, Hawai'i's *montane* (mon-TANE), or mountain, rainforests provide some of the best remaining habitat for native forest birds, and for hundreds of native insect species that live there too.

BOGS

Amidst the islands' rainforests are open areas where, instead of tall trees, everything grows small. These *elfin* forests of midget-sized trees are located in bogs where there is a lot of clay and the soil is poorly drained.

'Ōhi'a lehua trees grow 50 feet tall or even higher in the surrounding rainforest, but in the elfin forests they may be just a few inches to one foot in height. A close-up look around the miniature *'ōhi'a* trees may reveal some other interesting plants like the "toothbrush fern" that has tiny leaves with a little fringe on the tip.

Mikinalo, the sundew, is a reddish-pink plant just an inch tall. It is called a fly-catcher because any tiny insect that lands on a sundew will find its feet stuck in the sticky droplets of moisture that glisten from hairs over the leaf surface. The liquid slowly dissolves the insect, providing nutrients for the plant.

SUB-ALPINE FOREST

On Maui and the Big Island, tall mountains rise above the clouds. On the cold, high slopes of these mountains - Haleakalā, Mauna Loa, and Mauna Kea - there is not much rainfall. Here you will find Hawai'i's sub-alpine forests.

Māmane, a tree with bright yellow flowers and fern-like compound leaves, is the most abundant species. A small yellow bird, the *palila*, feeds only on the seed pods and flowers of this beautiful tree in the high elevation forest on the island of Hawai'i.

The higher you go up these mountains, the smaller the forest grows, until you reach shrublands with no tall trees. Several plants at these high elevations have grayish or silvery leaves, which offer protection by reflecting the intense sunlight. The best known of these is the silversword which grows on bare lava slopes on Maui and Hawai'i.

Alien Plants From Around The World

The Hawai'i we know today is a land of many cultures from around the world. As people came to Hawai'i from far places they brought with them the plants that were useful and important in their lives. Many plants that we think of as Hawaiian are actually alien species, introduced to the islands during the past two centuries. Hawaiian macadamia nuts came from Australia, Kona coffee from Africa. Mangoes came from India, lychee from China, while papayas, guavas, avocados, passion fruit, and pineapple were brought in from Central and South America. Even coconuts are not native to Hawai'i, but were introduced to the islands by early Polynesian voyagers.

The flowers in Hawai'i's beautiful *lei* are mostly aliens as well: yellow and white ginger from Asia, plumerias from Tropical America, and carnations from the Mediterranean. Exotic Hawaiian floral displays

include anthuriums from South and Central America, protea from Australia, and bird of paradise from South Africa. Even Hawai'i's state flower was, at one time, the common red hibiscus that is native to China. Today, it is *ma'o hau hele*, a native yellow hibiscus.

Some of Hawai'i's forests are made up entirely of alien trees. During earlier parts of this century, native forests of *koa* and *'ōhi'a* were sometimes bulldozed to make way for planting trees that were thought to be more useful to people. Many kinds of pine trees, fir trees and eucalyptus were planted as forests and still grow throughout the islands. But today, people no longer try to replace native trees with aliens because foresters have realized that native trees such as *koa* are far more valuable than pines and eucalyptus. Also, Hawai'i's natural forests provide valuable habitat for plants, birds, and insects found nowhere else in the world.

banana (maiʻa)

taro (kalo)

breadfruit (ulu)

POLYNESIAN INTRODUCTIONS

The first alien plants were brought to Hawaiʻi by early Polynesian voyagers who sailed from the Marquesas Islands and Tahiti more than 1,500 years ago. Upon reaching Hawaiʻi the Polynesians found lush, pristine forests but they did not find many plants they needed for food, medicine, wood, rope, containers, tools, and clothing. Over the centuries, the early Polynesians introduced about 26 plants to provide the necessities of life. Many of these can still be seen, especially in the lowland forests on the windward side of the islands.

Food plants brought by the Polynesians included taro, yams, sweet potatoes, breadfruit, and bananas. Among the medicinal plants were *noni* to help cure diabetes and reduce high blood pressure, *'ōlena* for ear aches and *'awa*, to relieve pain. Some Polynesian plants had several uses. *Kukui* trees, for example, provided medicine, food, dyes, and oil that was used for lamps (hence the name "candlenut" tree). The *ti* plant has a starchy root that can be cooked for food, and leaves that were used in religious ceremonies and made into rain capes, sandals, and food wrappers. Coconut trees were among the most useful of the Polynesian introductions. The leaves could be used for weaving, the trunks were made into drums, fibers from the husk were twisted into rope, the shell was used as a bowl, water inside the nut was good to drink and the coconut meat was used for food and oil.

coconut palm (niu)

ti (ki)

noni

goat
wild pig
cow
axis deer
sheep

Threats And Challenges

Hawai'i's natural forests have been shrinking or disappearing for centuries. About 40% of the islands' rainforests, 60% of the moist (*koa*) forests, and over 90% of the original dryland forests are now gone.

Fire destroyed much of the original forest cover. For hundreds of years, ancient Hawaiians used fire to clear the land. Today, fire is still a forest problem caused by careless smokers, untended campfires, sugarcane burning, military exercises, and vandalism. Shrublands, grasslands, and dryland forests have been especially hard hit by fire.

Feral mammals such as pigs, goats, cattle, deer, and sheep have caused much damage to Hawai'i's original forests. (*Feral* means domesticated animals that have gone wild.) When cattle were first introduced to the islands more than two centuries ago, they roamed the countryside and increased in numbers until there were tens of thousands of feral cattle. Thousands of feral goats also roamed the forests and shrublands. Because Hawai'i's native plants evolved without protective spines, thorns, bad tastes or poisons, the huge herds of cattle and goats easily ate the vegetation down to the ground. Erosion followed in their footsteps.

Alien plants have also done much harm to native forests. Plants such as banana poka vines and the ivy gourd cover the forest like a blanket; others such as kāhili ginger, strawberry guava, Koster's curse, and fire tree choke out native plants; and still others such as blackberry, lantana, and gorse form spiny thickets that you can hardly hike through.

Many scientists consider alien plants to be the greatest threat to Hawai'i's forests today, but other serious threats include insect pests, plant diseases, erosion and clearing forests for farming and other land use. Every threat, however, is also a challenge - an opportunity for people to work together to find ways to care for Hawai'i's remaining natural forests.

banana poka

strawberry guava

'ākohekohe

ko'oloa'ula

Moloka'i koki'o

palila

koki'o

ENDANGERED SPECIES

An endangered species is a type of plant or animal that is having a hard time surviving - a species that is in danger of becoming extinct, or vanishing forever.

Hawai'i has become our nation's capital for endangered species. In addition to the dozens of native bird species that have become extinct, nearly 40 are on the endangered species list. Several of these have not been seen for years, and are probably extinct. On Kaua'i, for example, five of the island's six endangered species of forest birds have not been seen since Hurricane Iniki struck the island in 1992. If they still survive, they occur in very small numbers

'ihi'ihilauakea fern

ʻōʻū

maʻo hauhele

tree snail

and are very close to extinction.

More than 200 species of Hawaiian plants are listed as endangered. More than 100 of these species have less than 40 individual plants still surviving in the wild.

Scientists and conservation groups throughout Hawaiʻi are working to learn more about why species become endangered, and what can be done to save them. There are many different kinds of studies going on, such as observing the feeding habits of birds, studying diseases of birds and plants, surveying damage from feral mammals, learning about the habitats of endangered species and where they occur, collecting seeds from rare plants, and exploring how to control alien species. One of the most important steps in saving Hawaiʻi's endangered species is what you are doing right now: learning about them.

ālula

Hibiscadelphus

CARING FOR OUR FORESTS; WHAT YOU CAN DO TO HELP.

DO clean your shoes, socks, other clothing and backpack carefully to remove clinging seeds after hiking. Use a stiff brush to scrub off dirt or dried mud because it may carry seeds that you can't see.

Don't ever leave an outdoor fire untended; put out campfires completely. Forest fires often begin when a campfire or other intentional fire gets out of control.

DO become involved with a school group or club with a forest stewardship project. Stewardship means working to care for the environment.

Don't smoke cigarettes. Not only are cigarettes bad for your health, but discarded cigarette butts are the cause of many forest fires.

DO help with projects such as weed-pulling and tree planting.

DO learn about our forests and their many challenges. Tell your teacher you would like to study Hawaiian forests in class. There are many excellent learning resources, especially one called the ʻŌhiʻa Project for teachers and students in kindergarten through eighth grade.

DO get a hiking book or map from the DLNR Division of Forestry and Wildlife or Division of State Parks. It will start you on your way to discovering the wonderful world of Hawaiʻi's natural forests.

Glossary

adaptive radiation a type of evolution where many species evolve from one ancestor; Hawai'i's honeycreepers, tree snails, and silversword relatives are examples.

alien species plants or animals that are not native to Hawai'i, but were brought to the islands by people.

ambush to capture by hiding in wait.

archaeologist a scientist who learns about the lives of ancient people by studying the materials they left behind.

bog an area of low-growing plants on wet, spongy soil.

canopy the upper layer of the forest where tree tops grow together, and create shade for the forest below.

carnivorous an animal that eats flesh.

decompose to break down in decay; to rot.

endangered species plant or animal species that are having a hard time surviving, and are in danger of becoming extinct.

endemic a plant or animal that lives naturally only in a limited area.

entomologist a scientist who studies insects.

epiphyte a type of plant that grows on another plant (but it doesn't take nutrients from the plant it grows on).

evolve when a type of plant or animal gradually changes into a new species over a long period of time.

feral domesticated animals such as pigs, goats, and sheep that have gone wild.

groundwater water within the earth that supplies wells and springs.

habitat the natural home of plants and animals.

honeycreepers a group of Hawaiian forest birds with very different beak shapes and sizes that all evolved from one ancestor.

liana high-climbing vines found in tropical rainforests (but not in native Hawaiian forests).

lichen — a type of plant that is actually two plants living together - algae and fungus - that grows as a crust on trees, rocks, and soil.

mesic — the moist forest zone, located on mountain slopes between dryland forest and rainforest.

native — plants or animals that live naturally in a place, and were not brought there by humans.

nectar — sweet honey-like substance produced by flowers to attract bees and birds.

pollinate — to transfer pollen (tiny dust-like particles) to the female part of a flower; the pollen will combine with the ovule, or egg, which then becomes a seed.

pristine — pure and unchanged, natural.

pioneers — the first to come to, or inhabit, an area; people are pioneers, but so are other plants and animals.

shrub — a woody plant that is smaller than a tree; a bush.

species — a group of plants or animals that have characteristics in common, and can interbreed.

stewardship — to actively care for the environment.

sub-alpine — the mountain zone below the alpine region. Alpine is the high mountain zone above the timberline, where trees don't grow.

vandalism — doing thoughtless harm or damage.

understory — the middle layer of a forest made of smaller trees and shrubs growing under the canopy.

INDEX

ʻaʻaliʻi 12
ʻakiapōlāʻau 19
alien plants 32, 34, 37
alien species 32, 33, 39, 42
alpine 24, 25, 43
ʻamakihi 18, 19, 28
anthuriums 33
ʻapapane 19, 29
avocado 32
ʻawa 35
banana 7, 34
banana poka 37
bat, Hawaiian 8, 14
bird of paradise 33
blackberry 37
bogs 13, 30, 42
breadfruit 34, 35
butterfly
    Blackburn's 8, 14, 15
    Kamehameha 9, 14, 15
carnations 32
caterpillar, carnivorous 3, 15, 42
cattle 12, 36
coconut 7, 35
coffee 32, 33
deer 36
dryland forest 13, 24, 25, 26, 27, 36
ʻelepaio 8, 20, 28
elfin forest 30
endangered species 27, 38, 39, 42
endemic species 7, 8, 14, 16, 42
epiphytes 29, 42
eucalyptus 33
evolution 7, 8, 13, 16, 19
ferns 4, 5, 10, 11, 22, 29, 30
fire, wildfire 12, 36, 42
fungi 8, 22
ginger 32, 37
goats 36

gorse 37
grasslands 24, 25, 26, 36
greensword 13
guava 7, 32, 37
hapuʻu ʻiʻi 10
Hibiscadelphus 27, 39
hibiscus 27, 33
honeycreepers 13, 19, 22, 42
ʻiʻiwi 8, 13, 18, 19, 20, 28
iliau 26
ivy gourd 37
kahuli 17
kauila 27
koa 18, 20, 22, 24, 28, 33, 36
kokiʻo 27, 38
koʻokoʻolau 12
Koster's curse 37
kukui 27, 35
lantana 37
lei 12, 20, 32
lichen 4, 5, 42
lobelia 12, 13
macadamia nuts 32
māmaki 14
māmane 24, 31
mamo 19, 20
mango 7, 32
maʻo hau hele 33, 39
medicinal plants 35
mesic forest 24, 25, 28, 36, 42
mikinalo 30
mosquito 14, 29
mosses 8, 10, 11, 19, 22
noni 35
ʻōhelo 4, 5
ʻōhia lehua 4, 5, 8, 18, 24, 29, 30, 33
ʻōlapa 8, 29
ʻōlena 35
ʻōʻō 20, 27

ʻopeʻapeʻa 14
ʻōʻū 8, 19, 20, 39
palila 19, 31, 38
papaya 7, 32
passion fruit 32, 33
pigs 36, 43
pili grass 26
pinao 14, 15
pine trees 33
pineapple 12, 26, 32
pioneer plants 6, 7, 42
plumeria 32
Polynesians 7, 34, 35
protea 33
pūkiawe 12
pulelehua 14, 15
pupu kani oe 17
rainforest 7, 13, 22, 24, 25, 28, 29, 30, 36, 43
seeds 5, 6, 11, 19, 41
sheep 36, 43
shrublands 12, 24, 25, 26, 31, 36
shrubs 7, 12, 13, 22, 28, 42
silversword 12, 13, 31, 43
snails 8, 16
    Carelia 16, 17
    singing tree 17, 39
spider, happy-face 8, 14, 15
spores 6, 11
sub-alpine forest 24, 25, 31, 43
sundew 30
taro 34, 35
ti 35
toothbrush fern 30
tree cottons 27
ʻuhaloa 12
uhiuhi 27
wiliwili 26, 27
yams 35

www.ingramcontent.com/pod-product-compliance
Lightning Source LLC
Chambersburg PA
CBHW041120300426
44112CB00002B/44